Inventin
Telephone

By Sue Graves

Long ago there were no telephones.
Instead people used a telegraph
to communicate. The telegraph sent
electricity through wires.

Telegraph operators used
this part of the telegraph
to send messages.

Electricity from the telegraph
made clicks. The clicks stood for
letters. Telegraph operators knew
how to turn the clicks into messages.

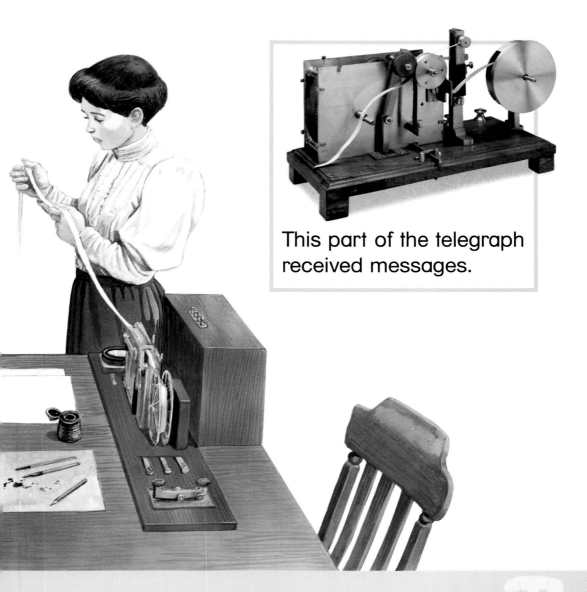

This part of the telegraph
received messages.

Alexander Graham Bell was interested in the telegraph. He thought he could make the telegraph better.

Bell knew that electricity from the telegraph made clicks. He thought that electricity could make voice sounds, too.

Thomas Watson was Bell's helper.
One day he was fixing Bell's telegraph.
The machine made a noise. "Ping!"

Bell was in a different room. He heard the noise. It came through the wires. Now Bell was sure electricity could send voices through wires, too.

Bell and Watson's first telephone

Bell and Watson got to work. They started to make a machine that used electricity to send voices. It was the telephone.

Bell's first telephone did not work well.
Watson spoke into the telephone.
Bell could not hear him.

Bell and Watson kept trying. They drew pictures. They used the drawings to make a better telephone.

On March 10, 1876, Bell was working
on the new telephone. He wanted to tell
Watson something. "Mr. Watson,
come here. I want you!" he called.

Watson heard him through the telephone in the next room. The invention worked!

the first successful telephone

Bell and Watson traveled around the
United States with their new invention.
They showed people how to use it.

Over the years telephones have become much better. Many telephones don't need wires anymore. Today telephones can be used in many places.

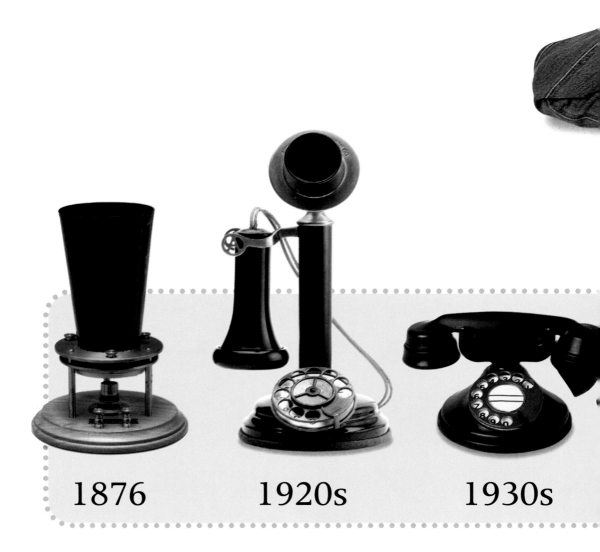

1876   1920s   1930s

1970s   1980s   2000s

Index